Cover Art And Work By Terry Urban
ISBN-13:
978-1516899975

ISBN-10: 1516899970

You And Me Under The Sea

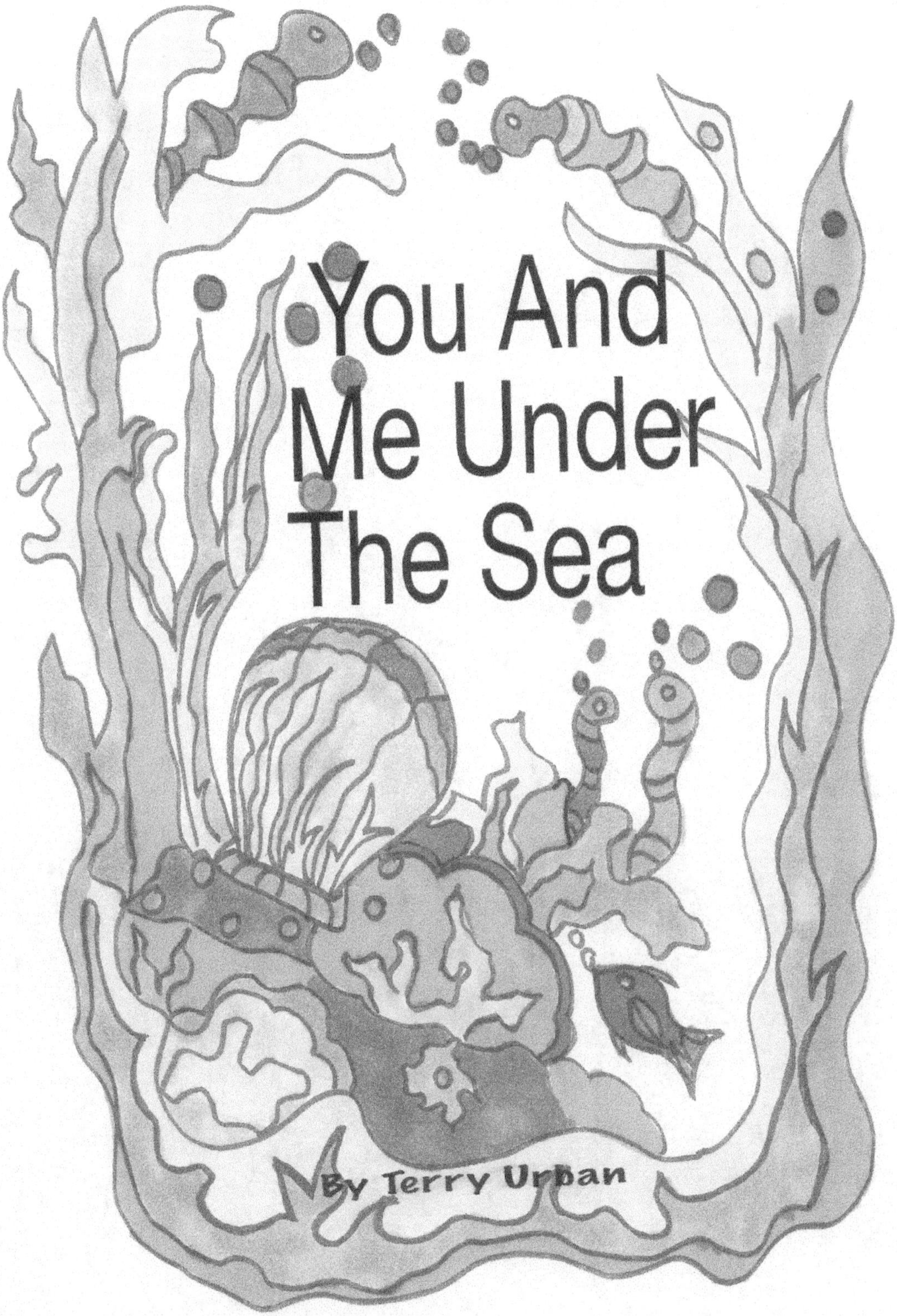

By Terry Urban

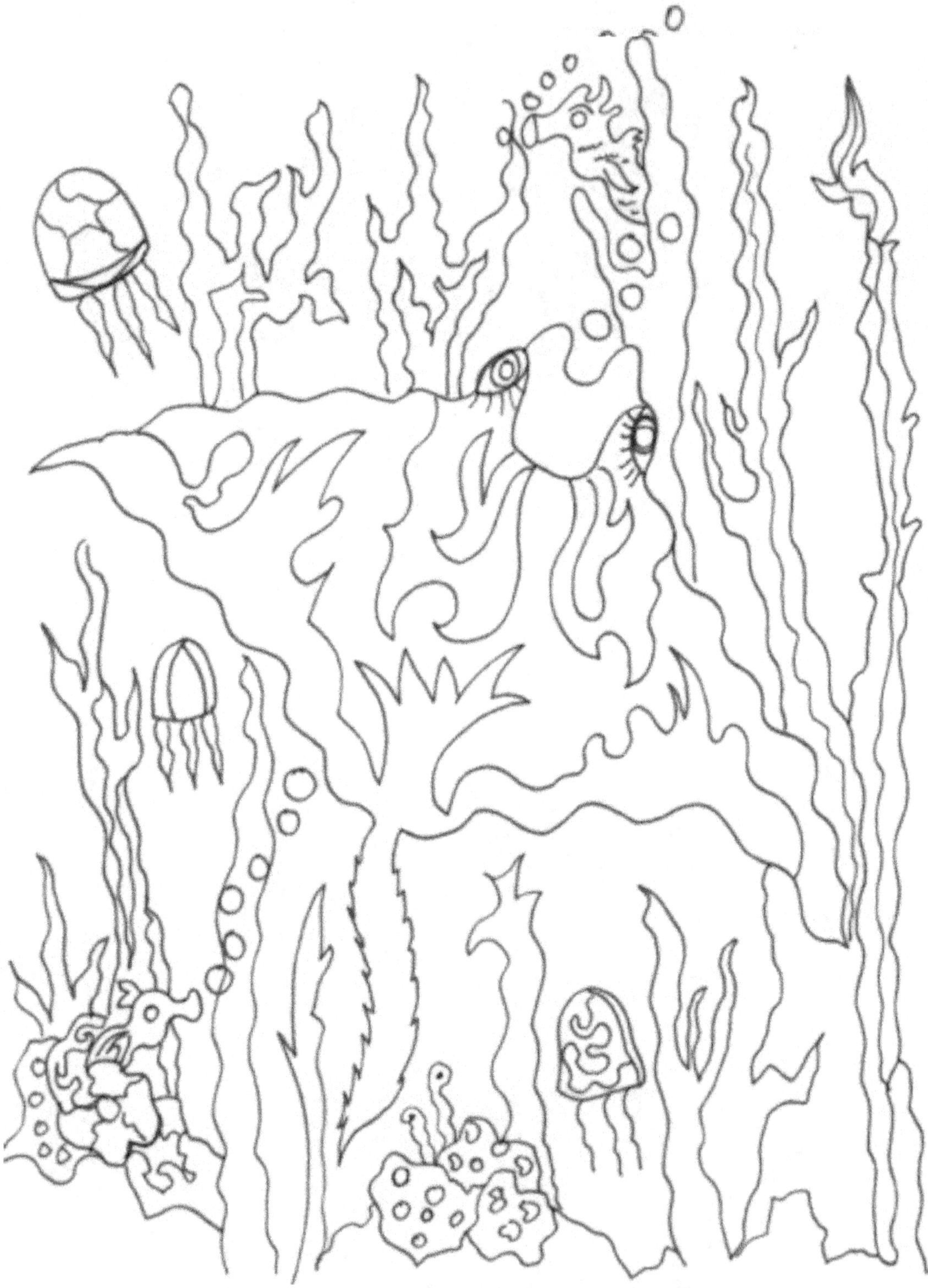

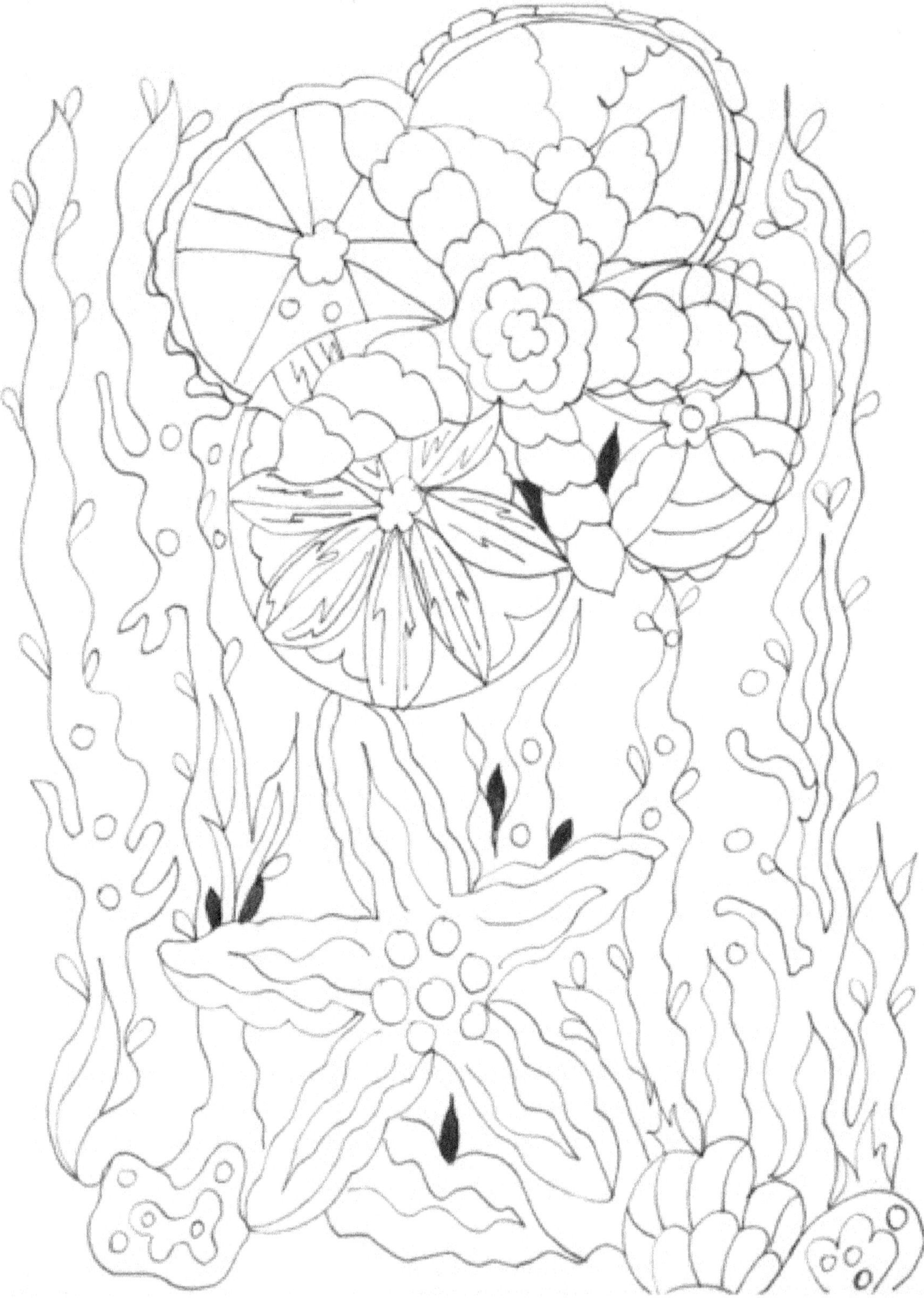

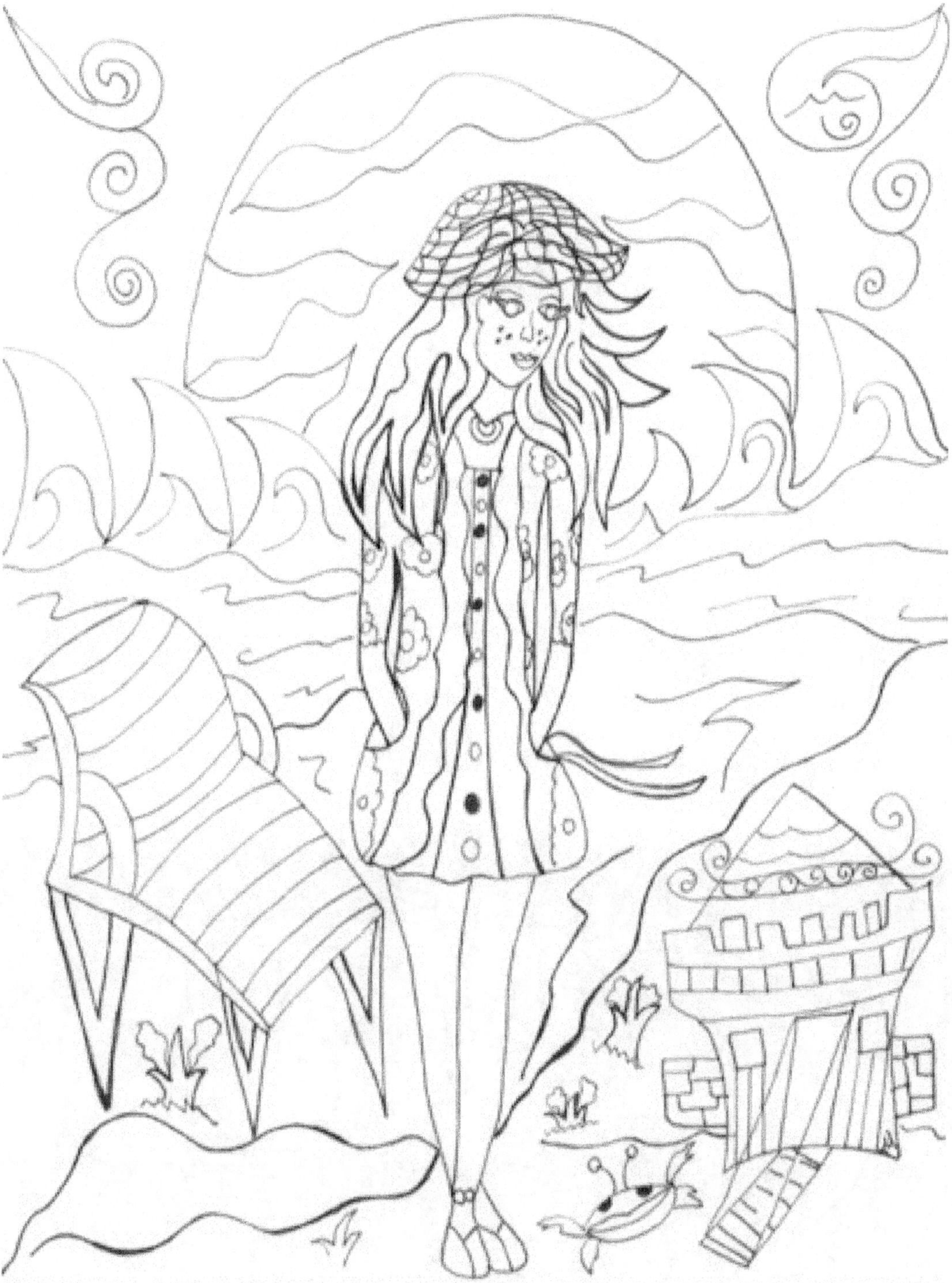

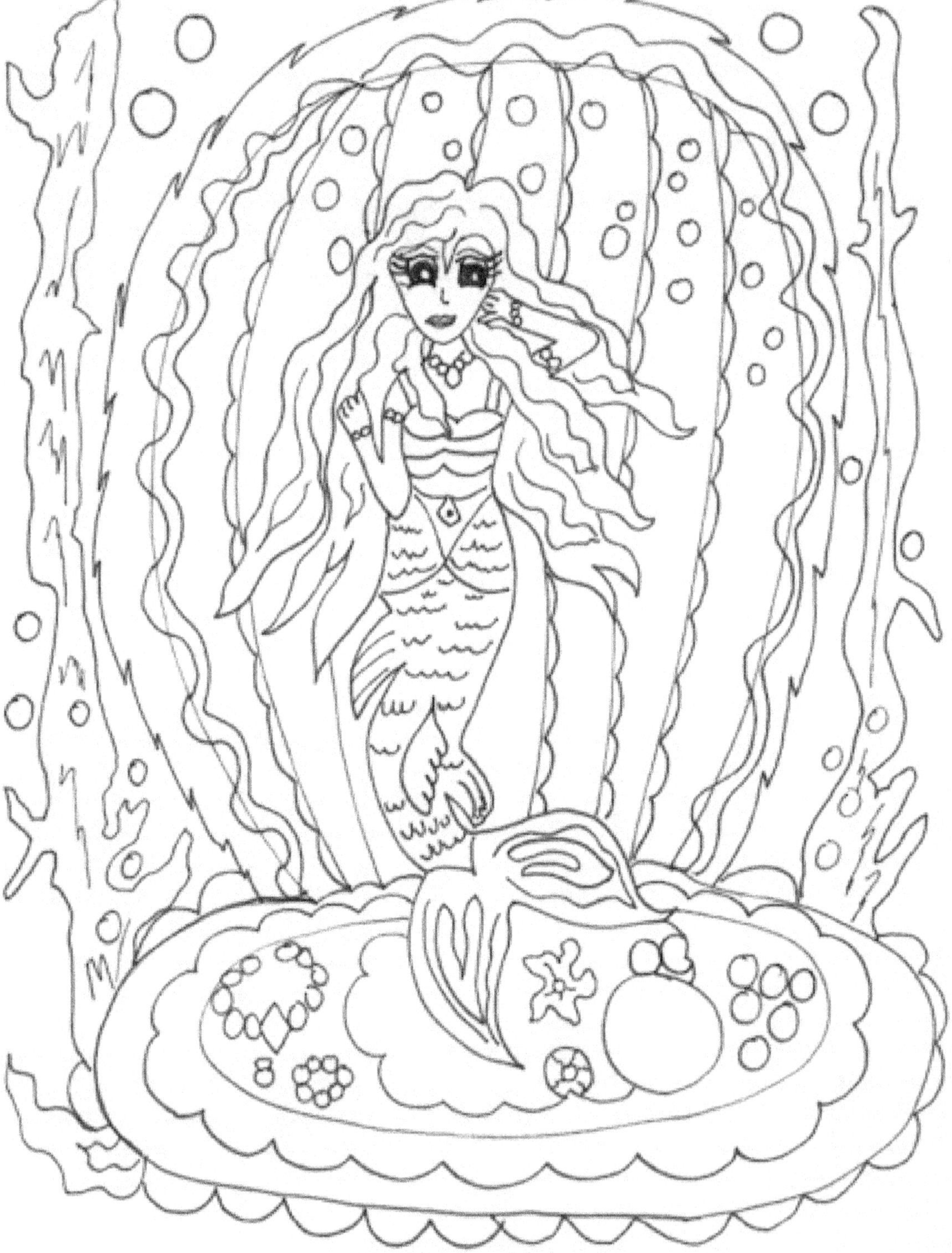

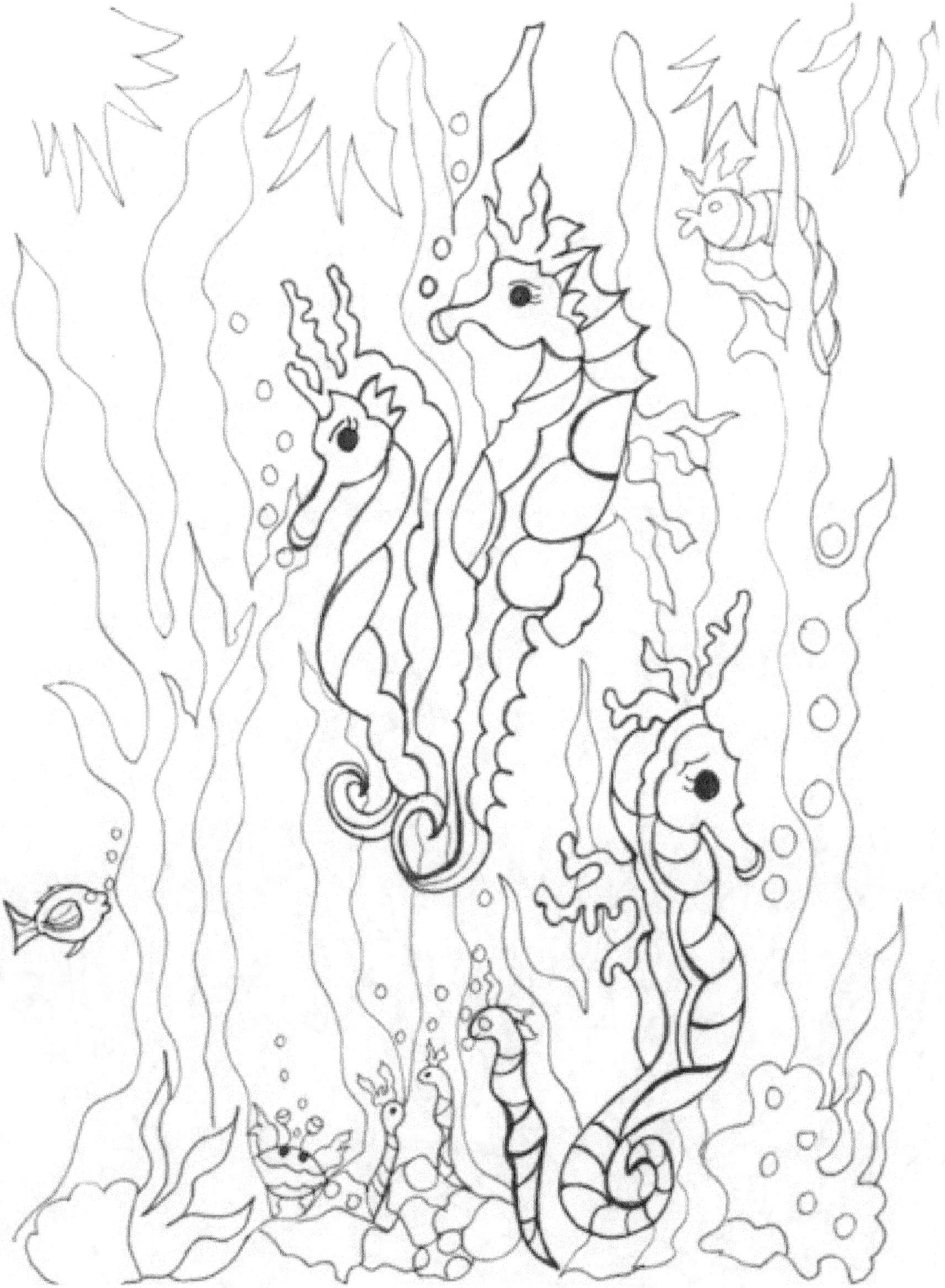

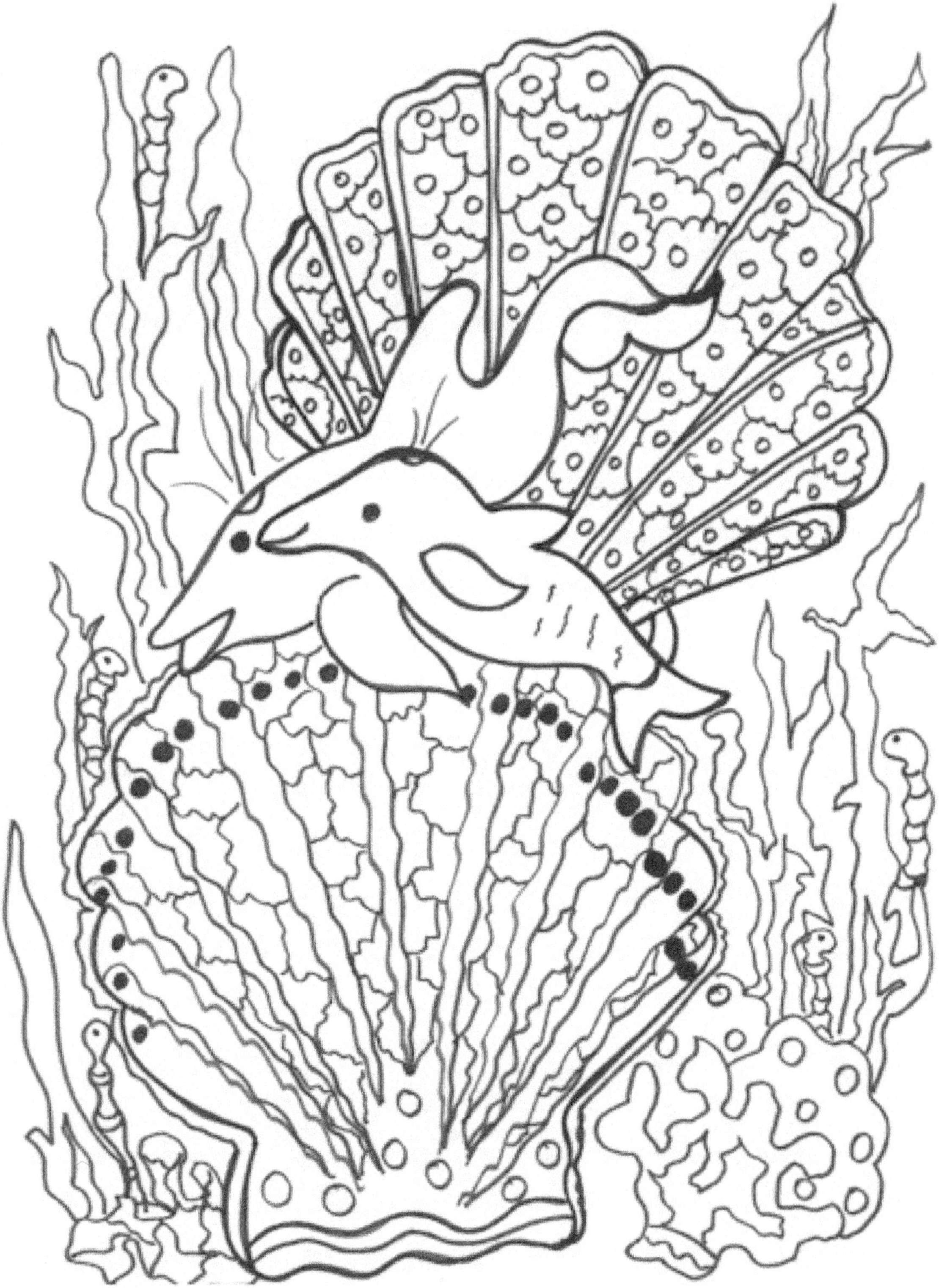

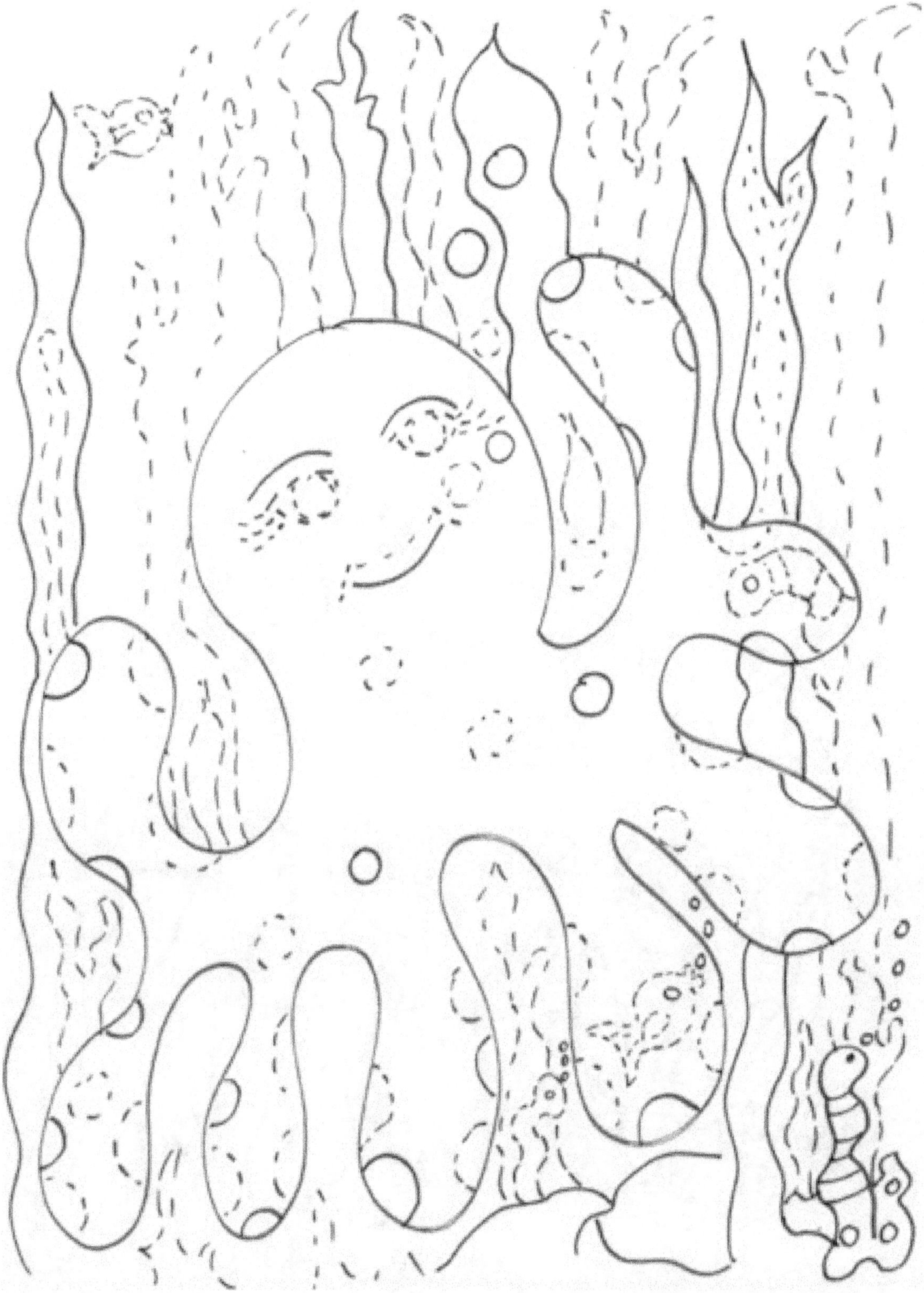

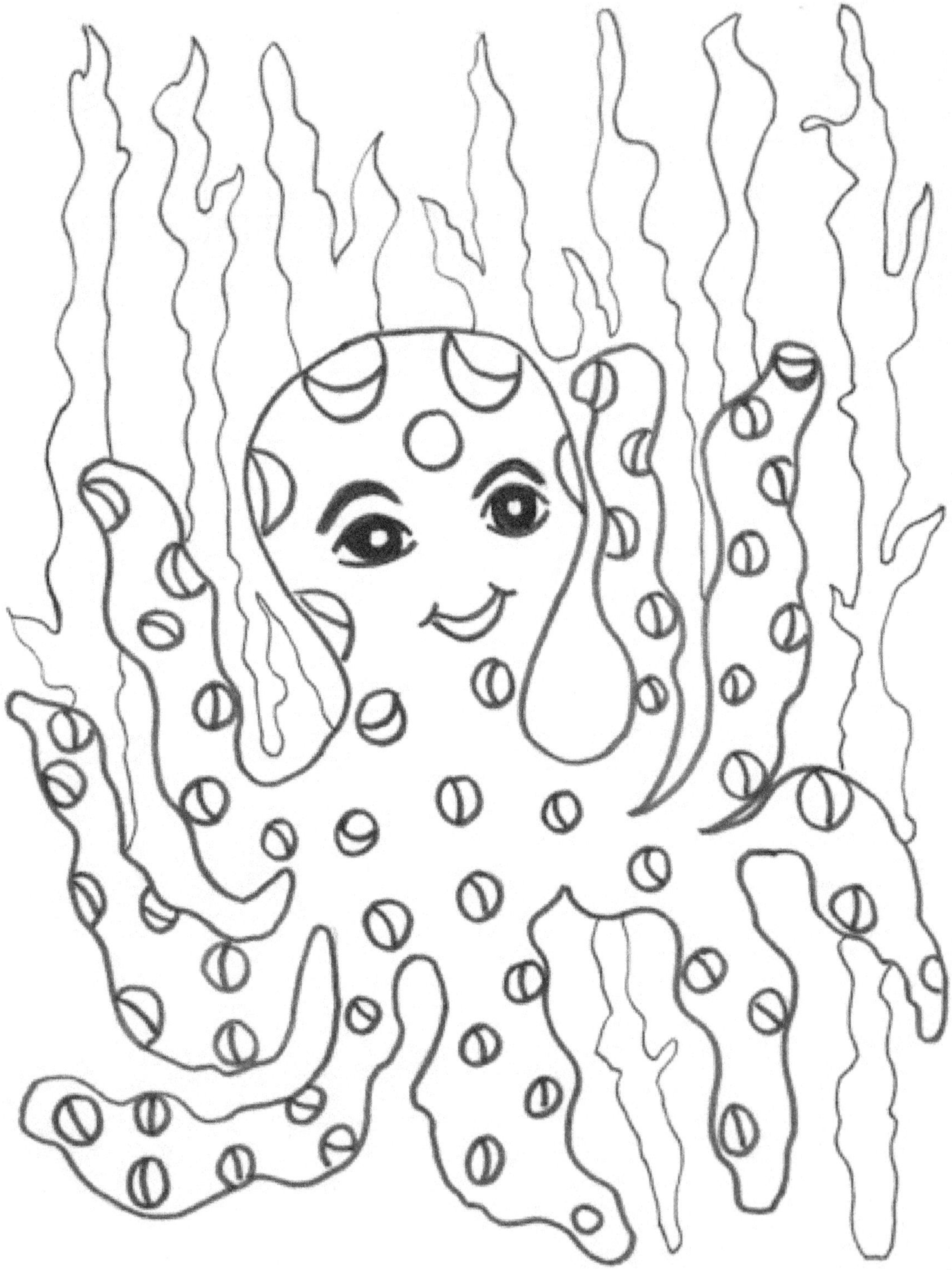

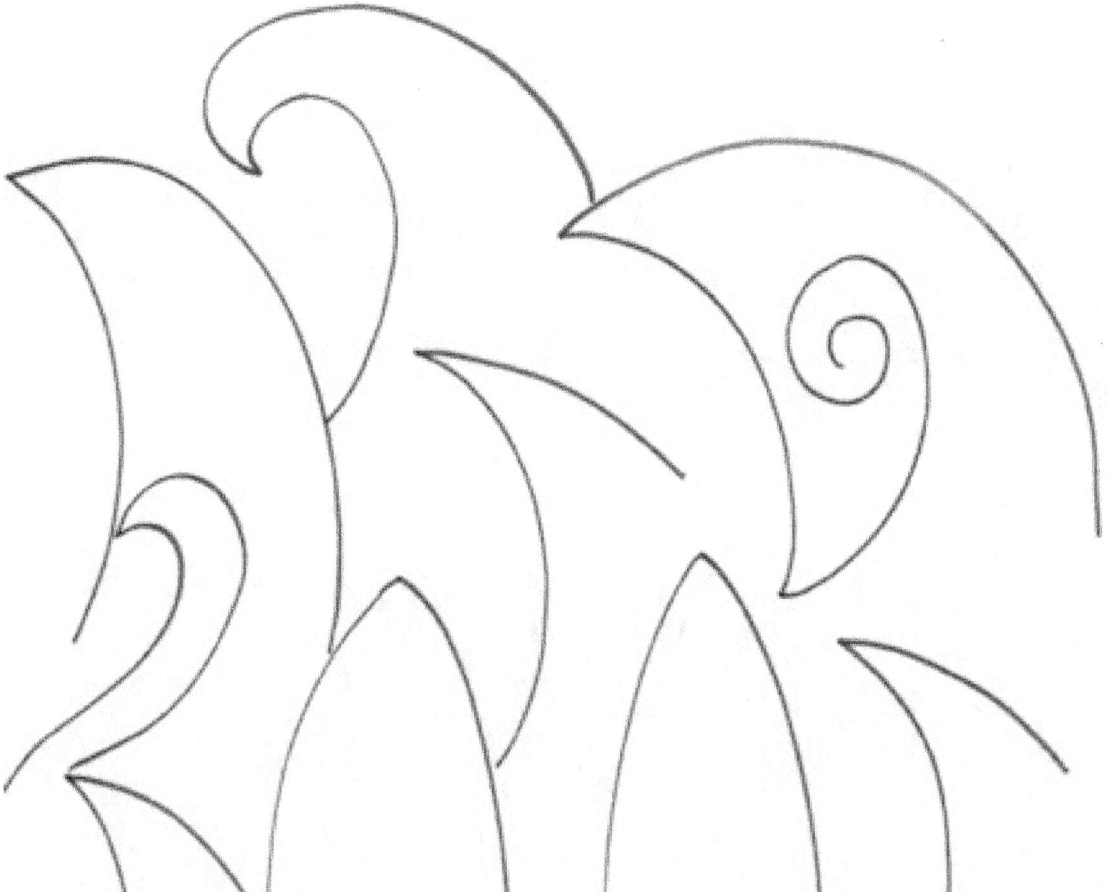

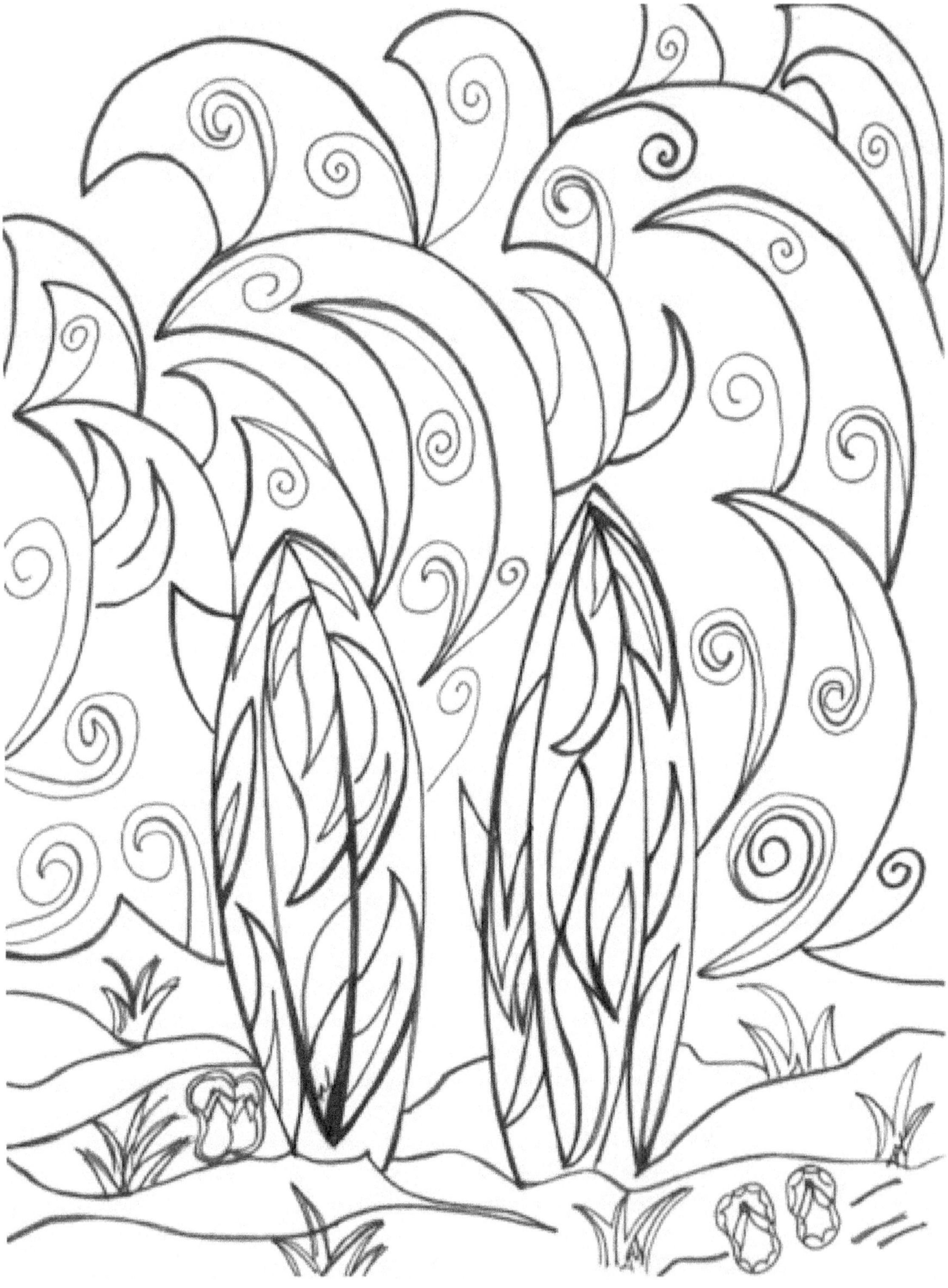

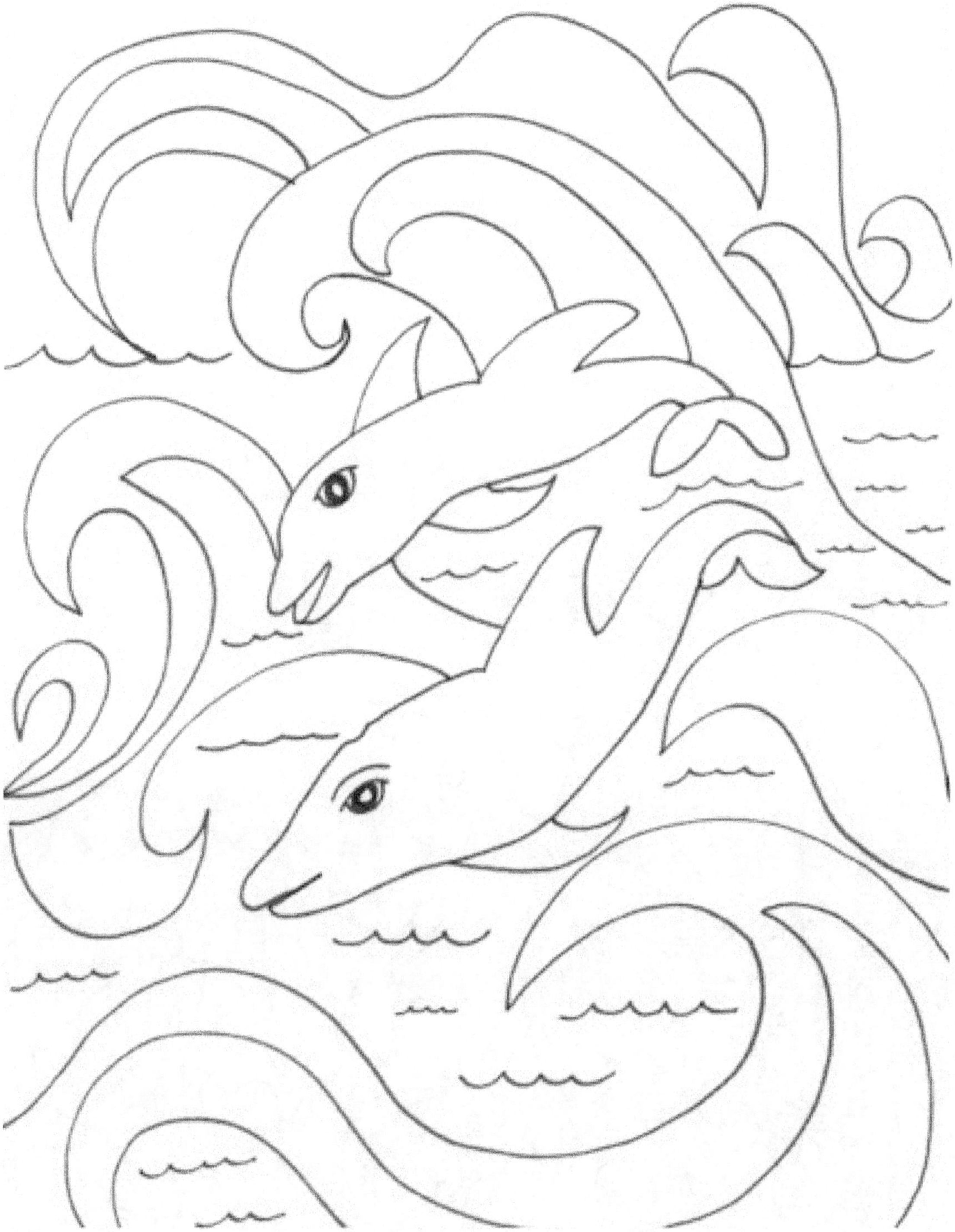

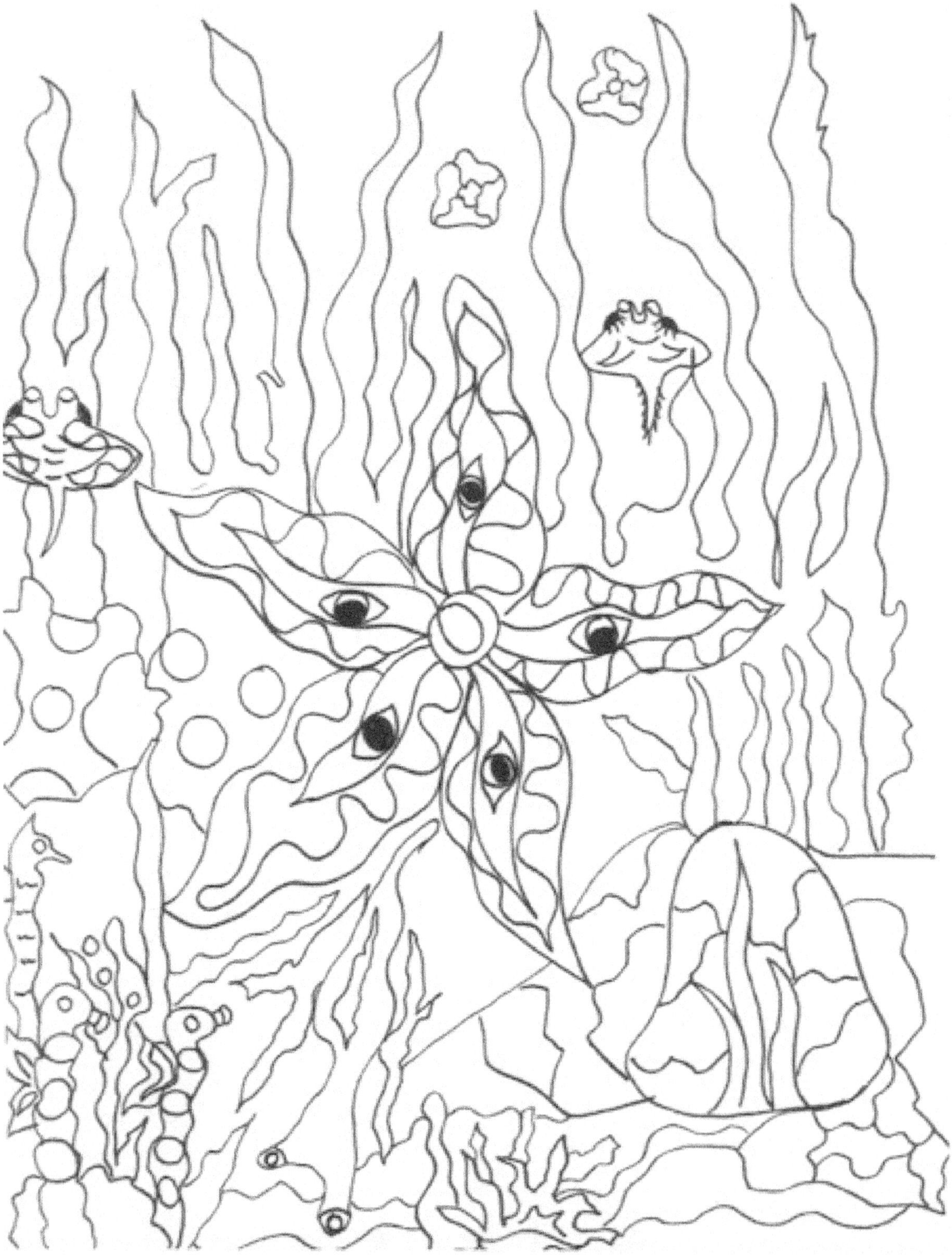

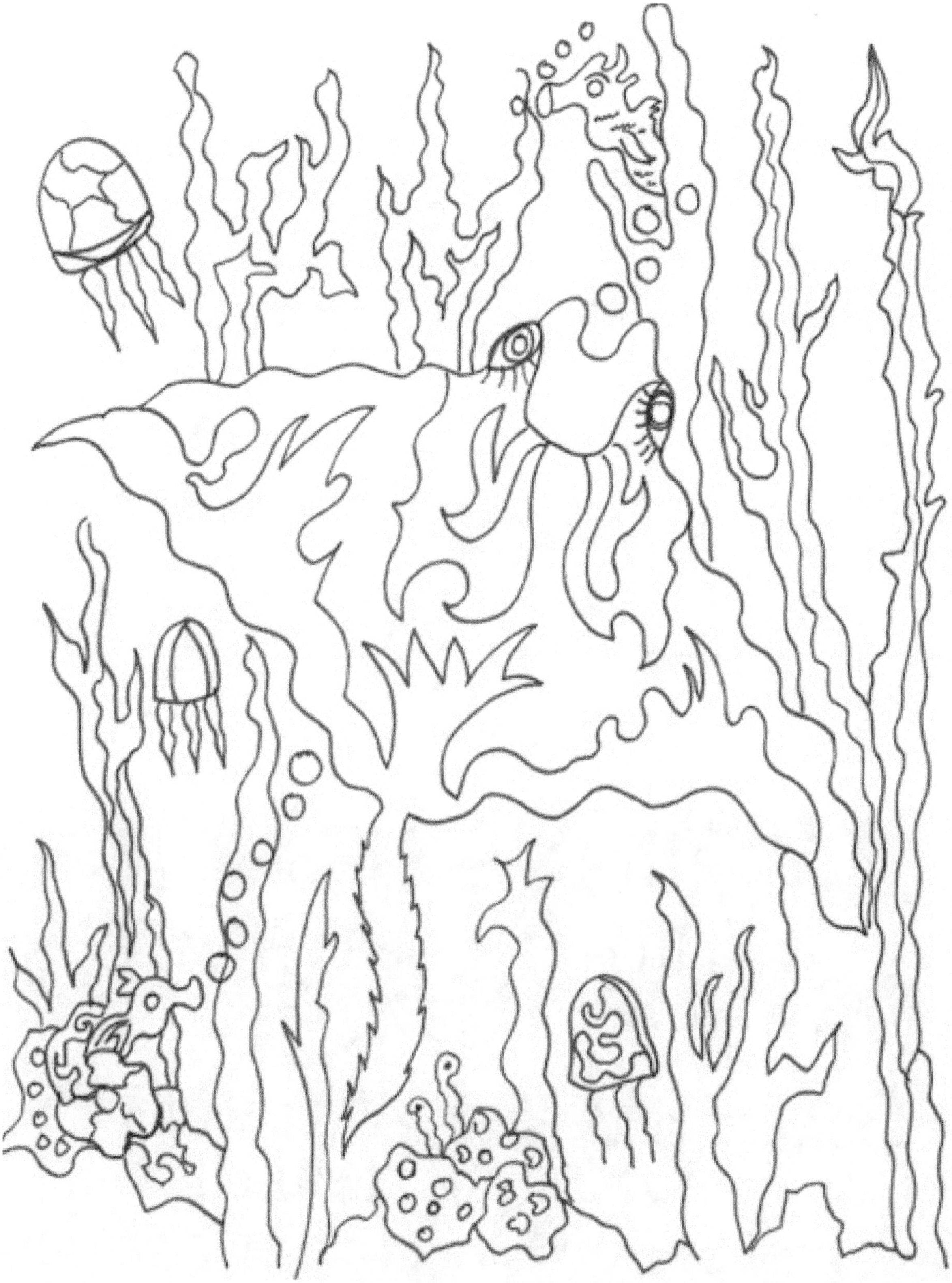

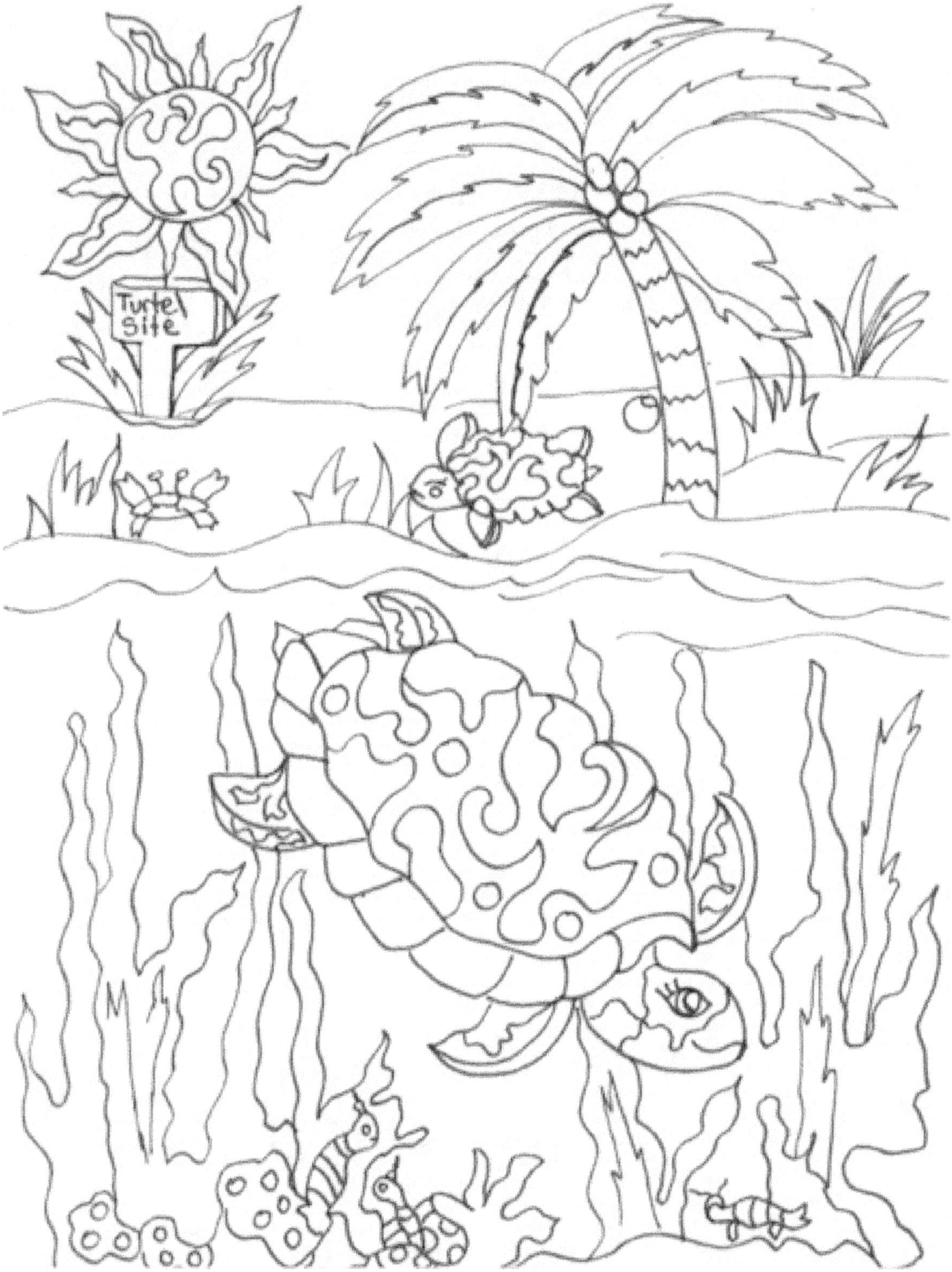
Turtel
Site

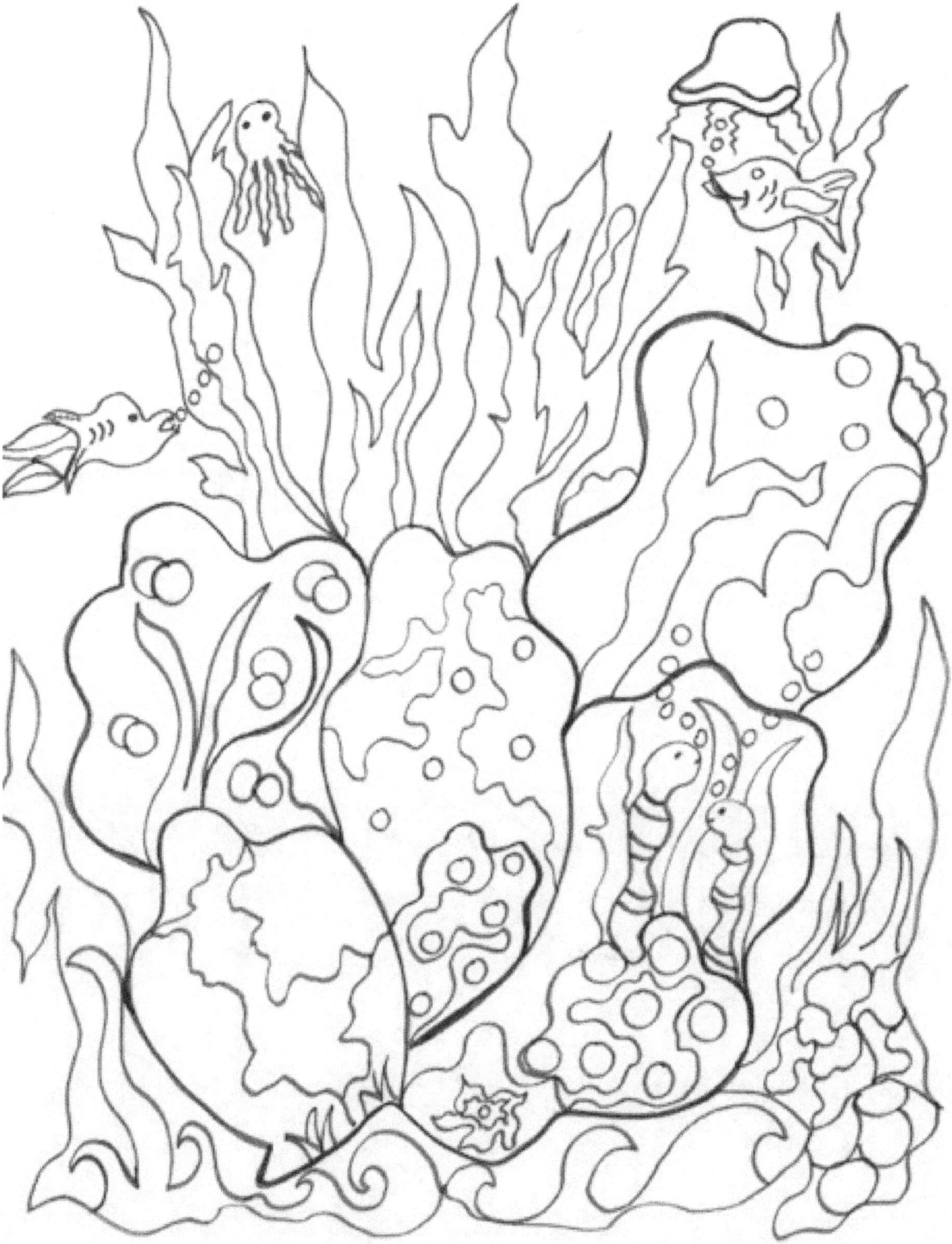

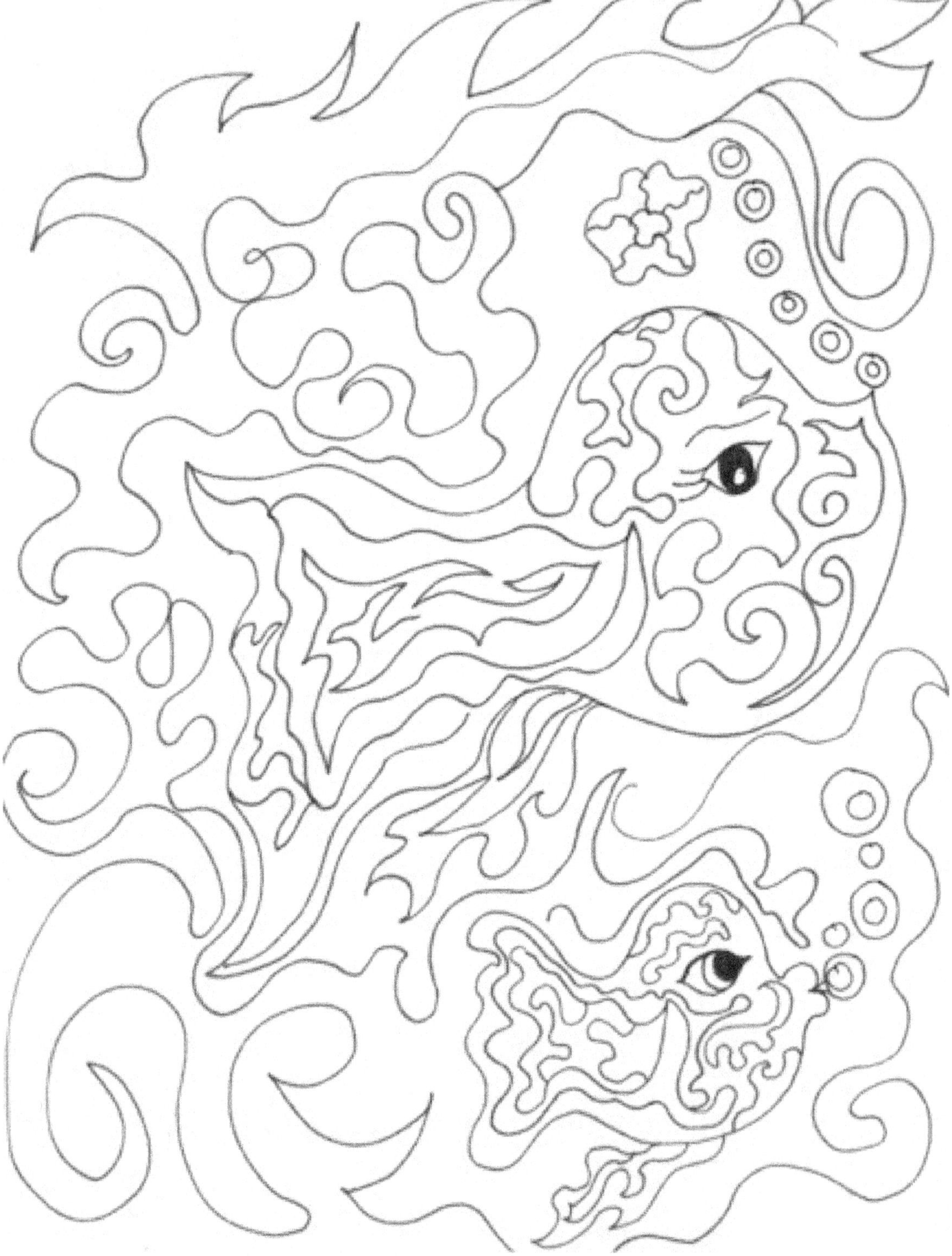

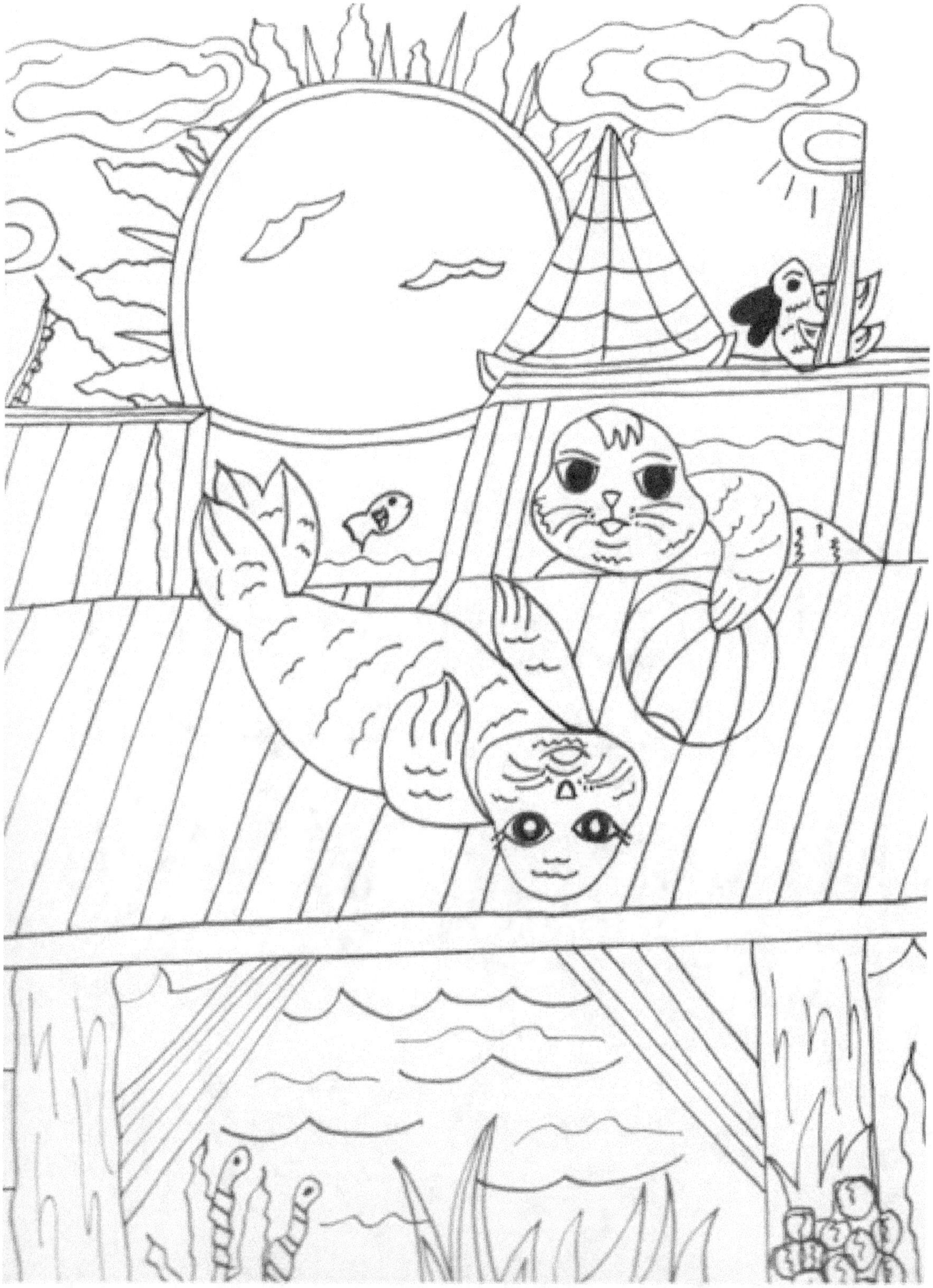

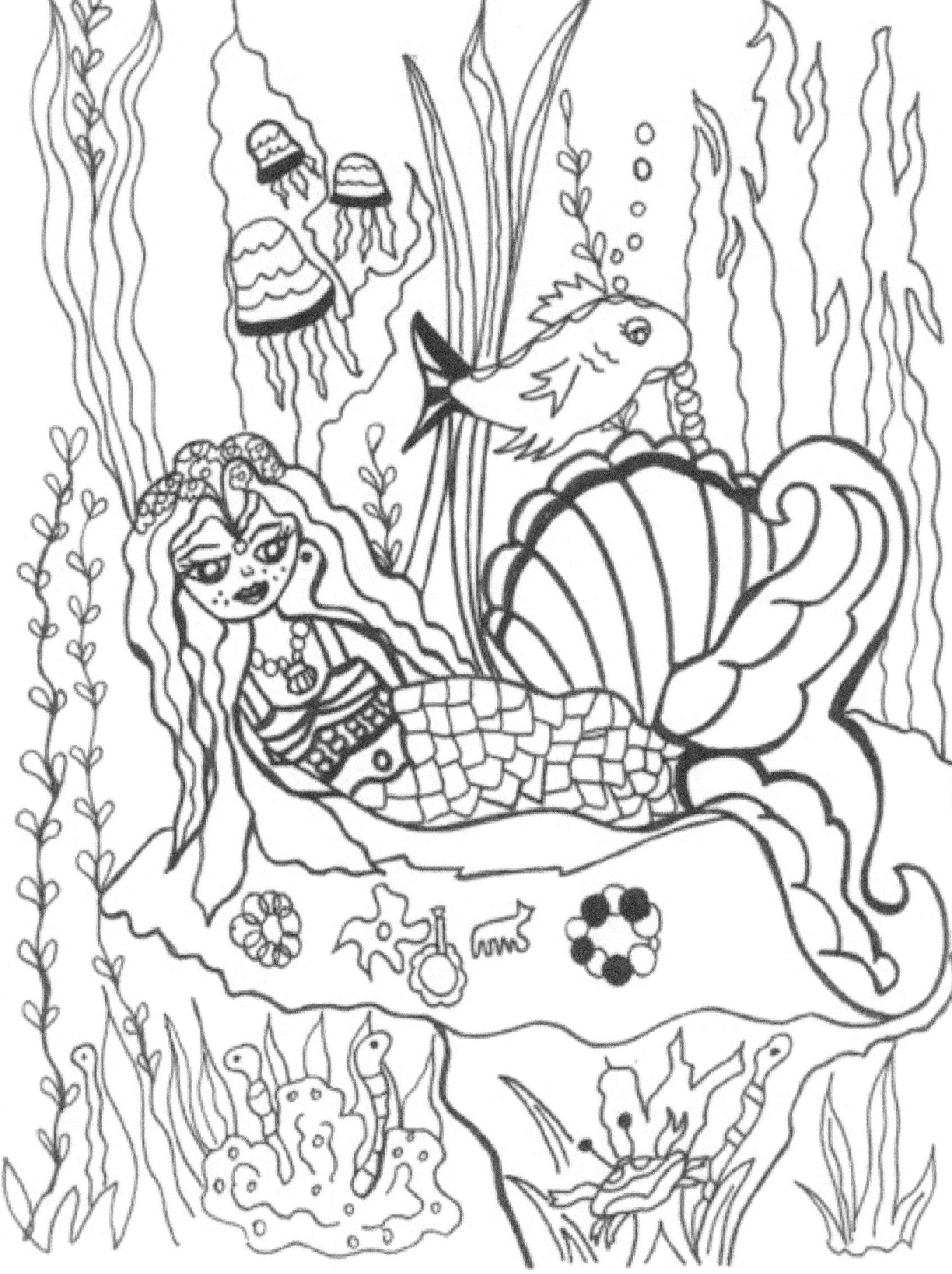

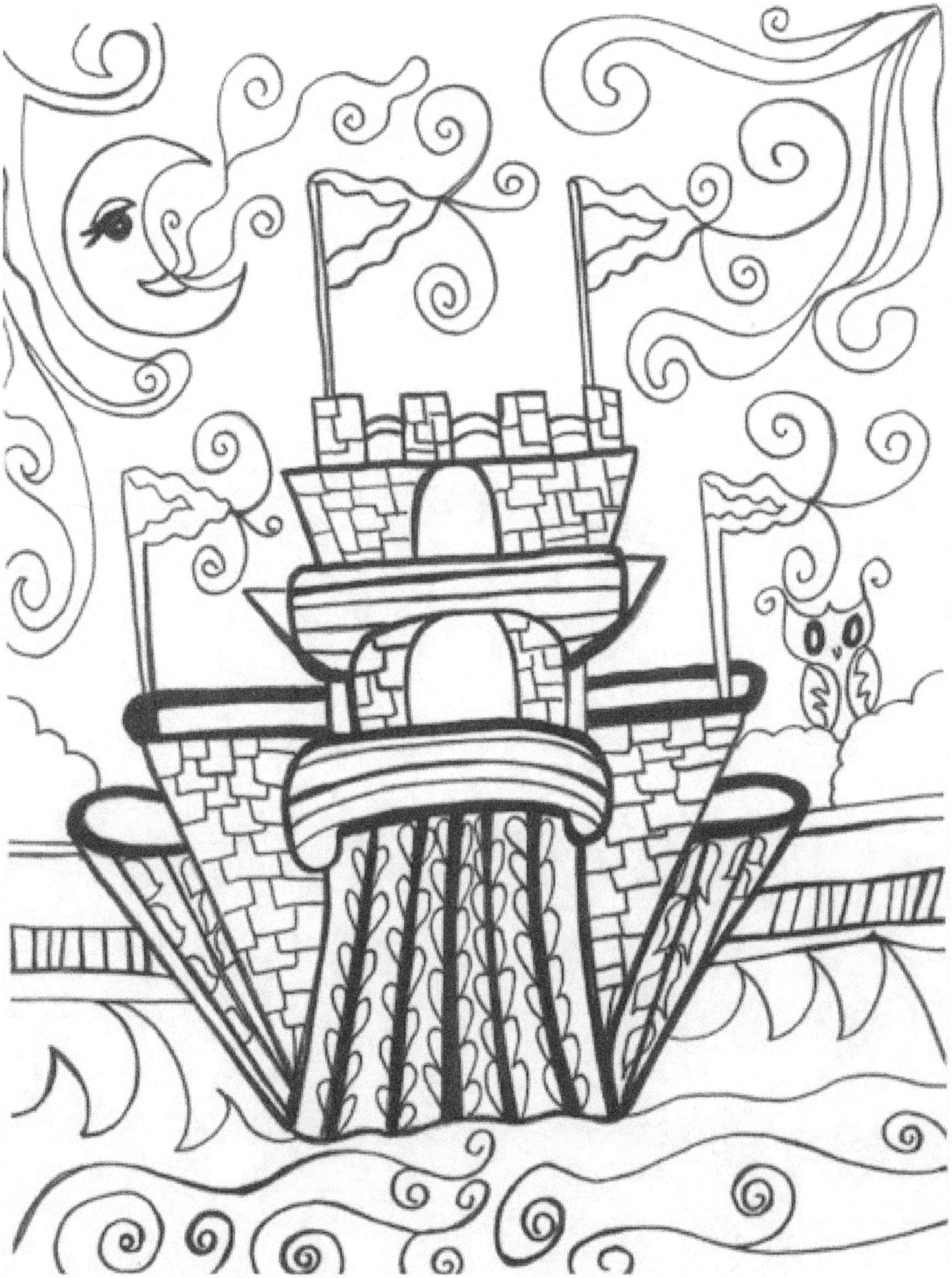

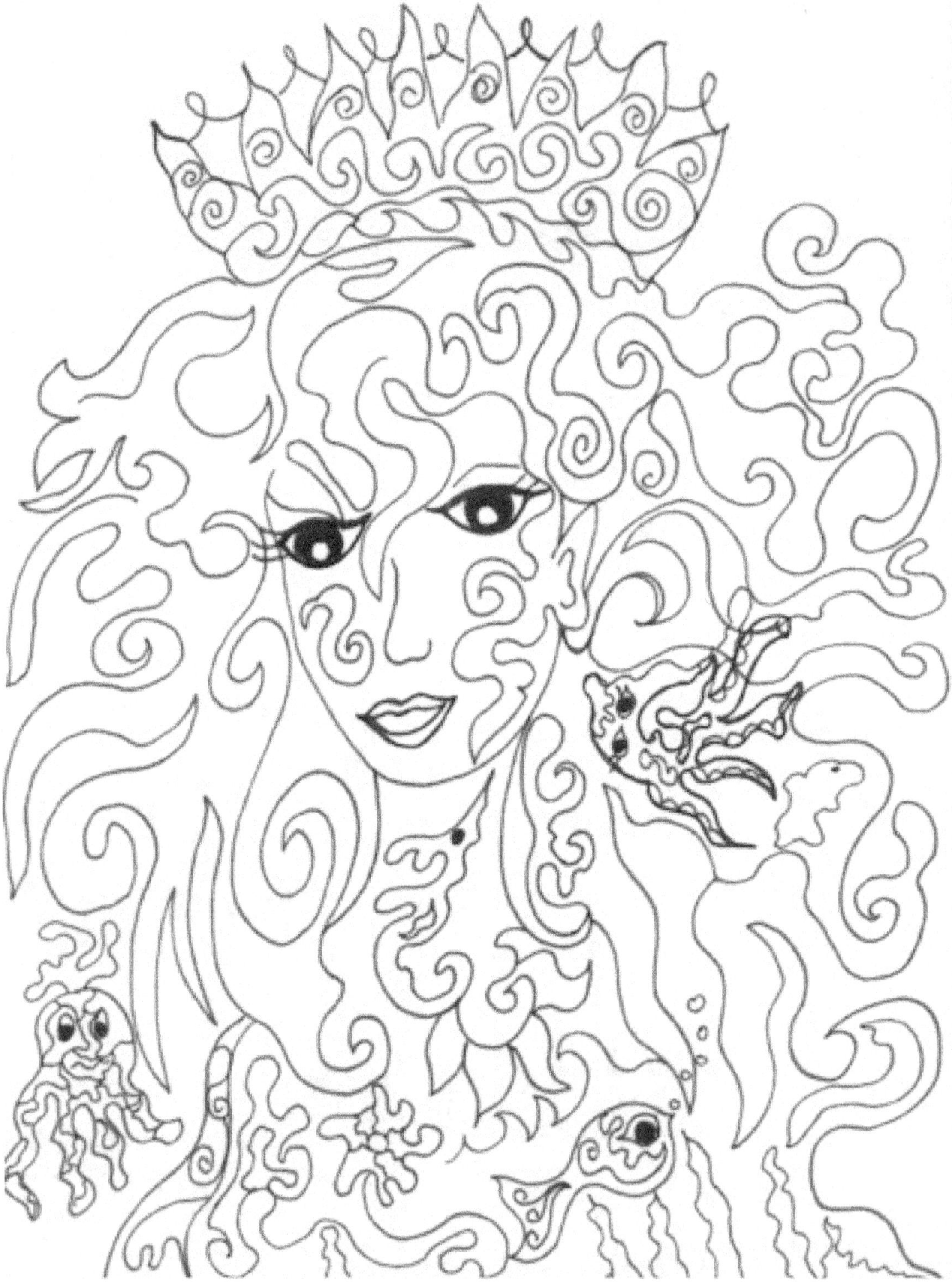

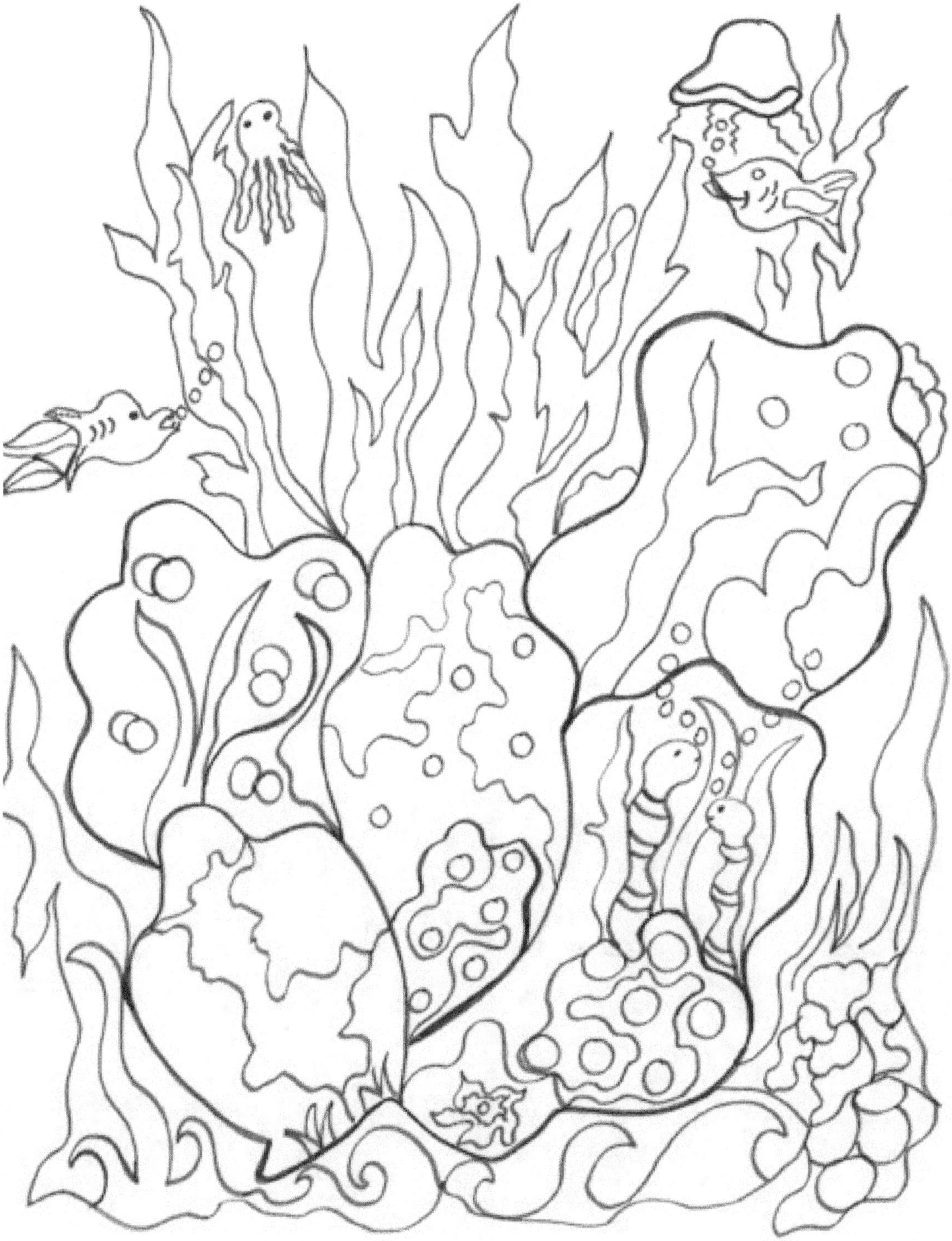

www.ingramcontent.com/pod-product-compliance
Lightning Source LLC
Chambersburg PA
CBHW080625180526
45168CB00007B/3060
9781516899975